EDGE
BOOKS

FANTASY
FIELD GUIDES

~ A FIELD GUIDE TO ~

Griffins, Unicorns,
and other Mythical Beasts

BY A. J. SAUTTER

CAPSTONE PRESS
a capstone imprint

Edge Books are published by Capstone Press,
1710 Roe Crest Drive, North Mankato, Minnesota 56003
www.capstonepub.com

Library of Congress Cataloging-in-Publication Data
Sautter, Aaron.
A field guide to griffins, unicorns, and other mythical beasts / by A.J. Sautter.
pages cm.—(Edge books. Fantasy field guides.)
Includes bibliographical references and index.
Summary: "Describes the features and characteristics of mythical creatures in a
quick-reference format"—Provided by publisher.
ISBN 978-1-4914-0690-8 (library binding)
ISBN 978-1-4914-0694-6 (paperback)
ISBN 978-1-4914-0698-4 (eBook PDF)
1. Animals, Mythical—Juvenile literature. 2. Griffins—Juvenile literature.
3. Unicorns—Juvenile literature. I. Title.
GR825.S278 2015
398.24'5—dc23   2014010194

Editorial Credits
Sarah Bennett, designer; Kazuko Collins, layout artist;
Kelly Garvin, media researcher; Katy LaVigne, production specialist

Photo Credits
The Bridgeman Art Library/Look&Learn/The BAL, 27; Capstone Press: Carlos
Molinari, 16, Jason Juta, 19, 21; Mike Nash, 1, 9, 22; Dreamstime: Dusan Kostic,
11, Solomandra, cover, 7; Science Source/Jacana, 14; Shutterstock: catmando, 13,
dalmingo, 28, Melkor3D, 4–5, 25

Artistic Credits
Shutterstock: argus, foxie, homydesign, Kompaniets Taras, Lora liu, Oleg
Golovnev, Picsfire, Rashevska Nataliia, xpixel

Printed in the United States of America in Stevens Point, Wisconsin.
052014   008092WZF14

Table of Contents

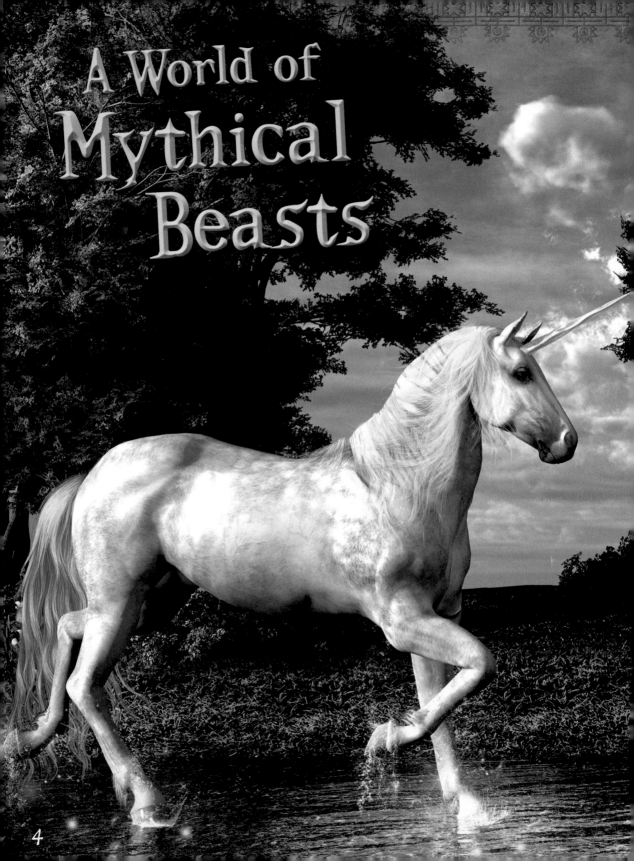

A World of Mythical Beasts

It's a magical and dangerous world out there. At least, that's what many ancient people believed. In many **myths** and legends, adventurers who explored the wild never knew what they would find. Heroes sometimes met powerful, yet friendly beasts such as griffins or phoenixes. But they were more likely to encounter deadly monsters such as minotaurs or chimeras. For many ancient people, fantastic creatures in stories were as real to them as eagles, lions, or whales are to us today.

Modern people know that mythical creatures like unicorns, harpies, and sea serpents live only in the imagination. Stories about these creatures have been around for thousands of years. And today they are as popular as ever. They keep popping up in modern books, movies, roleplaying games, video games, and more. Why is this? Maybe it's because these incredible beasts offer a sense of adventure that people rarely experience in real life.

Let's imagine for a while that mythical beasts are real and alive in the world today. If you wanted to find them, would you know where to look? How do these creatures live? What do they eat, and how do they behave? Get ready for a fantastic adventure as we look at amazing mythical creatures and how they'd live if they were real.

myth—a story from ancient times; myths often tried to explain natural events

5

Griffins

Size:
7 to 7.5 feet
(2.1 to 2.3 meters) long;
wingspan up to
20 feet (6 m)

Habitat:
dry caves in grassy hills
or mountain regions

Diet:
rabbits, sheep, deer, wild
horses, camels, buffalo

Life Cycle: Female griffins lay one or two large eggs every two years. The eggs hatch in about four months. Mothers feed and care for their young for about one year. At this point most young griffins are ready to begin flying and hunting for themselves. When griffins reach adulthood at about age 5, they set out to find **lairs** and mates of their own. Griffins usually live for about 35 years, but a few have lived up to age 50.

Physical Features: Griffins are a combination of features from two fierce hunters. Their upper bodies have the heads, wings, and razor-sharp **talons** of large birds of prey. Their lower bodies feature the powerful legs, claws, and tails of lions. A griffin's muscular body is usually covered with a mix of golden hair and feathers. Griffins can fly up to 50 miles (80 kilometers) per hour with their strong wings. They also have incredible eyesight and can spot a rabbit moving up to 3 miles (5 km) away.

Behavior: Griffins usually live alone and spend much of their time hunting for food. Although they don't speak, griffins show some intelligence. They can track prey over long distances. Occasionally they hunt in small packs to trap and kill large prey. Some griffins are friendly toward people. They may offer help when people are in need.

lair ⤙ a place where a wild animal lives and sleeps

talon ⤙ a long, sharp claw

7

Harpies

Size:
4 to 4.5 feet (1.2 to 1.4 m) tall; wingspan up to 9 feet (2.7 m)

Habitat:
rocky cliffs and small caves near the sea

Diet:
fish, crabs, seals, small birds; prefer humans when possible

Life Cycle: Harpies lay up to six eggs once per year. However, only two or three eggs will hatch successfully. After hatching, usually only one harpy chick survives to adulthood. Harpy mothers feed their young for about two months before forcing them out of the nest to care for themselves. Young harpies grow quickly and are considered adults by age 4. Nobody is certain, but it's thought that harpies can live up to 40 years.

Physical Features: Harpies have the bodies of large birds such as vultures or owls. They have large, powerful wings and strong scaly legs. Their feet are tipped with razor-sharp talons. Harpies' heads appear as hideous women. They have yellow eyes and long greasy hair. Their mouths are filled with decaying teeth. Harpies never bathe. They stink horribly from the bits of rotting flesh and filth that cover their feathered bodies.

Behavior: Harpies live alone, but they often hunt together in small flocks. They spend much of their time perched on rocky cliffs overlooking the sea to watch for prey. Harpies will eat almost any kind of meat, but they like human flesh best. In spite of their horrid appearance, harpies have beautiful singing voices. Harpies use their magical singing ability to cloud the minds of victims and draw them close before attacking.

Fact In one ancient Greek myth, harpies cause a lot of problems for King Phineas of Thrace. The god Zeus blinded Phineas for sharing too many of his visions of the future. Zeus then put Phineas on a deserted island with tables full of food. But Zeus allowed harpies to keep stealing the food before Phineas could eat it.

Phoenixes

Size:
10 to 12 feet
(3 to 3.7 m) tall;
wingspan up to
30 feet (9 m)

Habitat:
rocky cliffs in
mountain regions

Diet:
rabbits, sheep,
goats, deer,
camels, warthogs

Life Cycle: Phoenixes are extremely rare. They have the most unique life cycle of any known creature. Rather than laying eggs, these incredible birds go through an amazing change every 300 years. When a phoenix nears the end of its life, it builds a nest on the highest mountain peak it can find. When its time comes, it bursts into flame and its body burns to ashes. A short time later, a new phoenix chick emerges from the ashes. It's uncertain if these chicks are new birds, or if the old phoenix simply **regenerates** its old body. If this is the case, then phoenixes may live for thousands of years. It's unknown how many times these birds can be reborn.

Physical Features: When a phoenix becomes angry, its feathers begin glowing red with fire. This trait may be why phoenixes are also called firebirds. Phoenixes are very strong. They could carry an adult elephant if they wished. Phoenix tears have magical healing qualities. They can heal serious wounds in a matter of seconds. Phoenix feathers also have magical properties. Wizards often used them to make their magic wands more powerful.

Behavior: Phoenixes are private creatures that prefer to live far from humans. These mysterious birds are good and noble. They'll do whatever they can to fight against the forces of evil. In rare cases phoenixes have become loyal friends to good wizards. They will come to their friends' aid whenever they are called.

regenerate ⟶ to make new

Pegasi

Size:
8 to 8.5 feet
(2.4 to 2.6 m) long;
wingspan up to
25 feet (7.6 m)

Habitat:
forests and
grassy plains

Diet:
grass, oats, apples,
carrots, beets, and
other root vegetables

Life Cycle: A female pegasus gives birth to one **foal** about every five years. Mothers care for their young until they are fully grown. Foals are born without wings. The wings begin growing out at about age 2. A pegasus reaches adulthood at about age 4, or when its wings are strong enough for it to fly. The pegasus then leaves its mother and flies off to find its own territory. Most pegasi can live about 50 years, though a few have been known to live into their 70s.

Physical Features: Pegasi are very similar to horses. They have powerful bodies, strong legs, muscular necks, and noble faces. Their hair is usually white or light gray. Their powerful wings allow them to fly up to 50 miles (80 km) per hour. Their manes and tails are made of hair and feathers.

Behavior: Pegasi prefer living on their own in the wild. They enjoy their freedom and are not easily **tamed**. However, pegasi are as intelligent as humans and are good judges of character. They do not tolerate evil. If a wicked person tries to ride a pegasus, it will react violently and attack that person. However, if someone treats a pegasus with kindness and respect, it may become a loyal friend. It may even allow that person to ride it into battle.

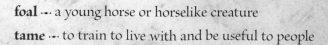

foal ⋯ a young horse or horselike creature
tame ⋯ to train to live with and be useful to people

★ ★ ★
FANTASY ALL-STAR

Pegasus is a famous creature in several ancient Greek myths. The winged horse carried the hero Bellerophon into battle to kill the monstrous Chimera. Pegasus then faithfully served the god Zeus on Mount Olympus. For his service, Zeus turned Pegasus into a constellation of stars to live forever in the night sky.

Fact Two unicorns are killed for their healing blood in the book *Harry Potter and the Sorcerer's Stone*. The evil lord Voldemort, who is near death, drinks the unicorns' blood to stay alive.

Unicorns

Size:
8 to 8.5 feet
(2.4 to 2.6 m) long

Habitat:
grassy clearings
in large forests

Diet:
grass, nuts, berries,
ferns, and other
leafy plants

Life Cycle: Unicorns are extremely rare. It's thought that these majestic creatures have only one foal about every 100 to 150 years. Unicorn mothers watch over their young for about 50 years, or until their horns are fully grown. Nobody is sure how long unicorns live naturally. But some people think they can live for more than 1,000 years.

Physical Features: Unicorns resemble large white horses, but they have some unique features. Unicorns usually have bright blue or violet eyes and have excellent eyesight. Unicorns are born a light gray or silver color. But as they age, they gradually lighten until they are pure white. Of course, a unicorn's most famous feature is the 2 to 3 foot (0.6 to 0.9 m) **ivory** horn that grows from its head. Unicorn horns have strong magical properties. They can be ground up and used to make strong healing potions or ointments. Some wizards even craft unicorn horns into powerful magic wands.

Behavior: Unicorns are intelligent creatures and are fierce protectors of their forest homes. They do not tolerate evil in any form. Unicorns can easily sense wicked people or creatures nearby. They will quickly attack to drive such creatures out of the forest. Unicorns normally live alone or with a mate deep in the forest. They want nothing to do with humans. But they are often friendly toward elves, fairies, and other creatures that respect nature.

ivory -- a hard, creamy-white material that makes up an animal's tusks or horns

Minotaurs

Size:
7.5 to 8 feet
(2.3 to 2.4 m) tall

Habitat:
mazelike networks of
underground caves;
tunnels and sewers
under ancient cities

Diet:
any kind of meat
including sheep, pigs,
goats, or goblins;
prefer human flesh
whenever possible

Life Cycle: The first minotaurs were created by evil wizards who placed magical curses on people who angered them. Females have one child about every 20 years. Young minotaurs reach adulthood by about age 8. Minotaurs live violent lives and are often killed before they reach the age of 50. However, they sometimes live up to 300 years.

Physical Features: Minotaurs are a strange combination of humans and bulls. Their heads and lower bodies are like a bull's while their arms and **torsos** are similar to a human's. Minotaurs' muscular bodies are covered in shaggy black or brown hair. These beasts also have hooves instead of feet. Minotaurs' gleaming yellow eyes give them excellent vision in the dark. All minotaurs have sharp, deadly horns used for attacking their enemies and prey.

Behavior: Most minotaurs live alone in mazelike caves or city sewers. These monstrous creatures spend most of their time prowling for their next meal. Minotaurs have an amazing sense of direction. They never get lost in their dark and twisted underground tunnels. This ability is a great advantage for minotaurs. It helps them hunt humans and other prey that wander into their mazelike homes.

torso -- the part of the body between the neck and waist, not including the arms

Chimeras

Size:
about 6.5 feet (2 m) tall; up to 15 feet (4.6 m) long

Habitat:
dry caves in hilly regions

Diet:
deer, sheep, rabbits, wild pigs; can eat grass and other plants, but prefer meat

Life Cycle: Chimeras are not born nor hatched from eggs like other animals. They are instead the result of experiments performed by evil gods or wizards. All known chimeras are already adults. It's unknown how long these deadly creatures can live.

Physical Features: Chimeras are one of the strangest beasts imaginable. They are a combination of several creatures. Most chimeras have two heads—one of a lion and one of a goat. However, some chimeras also have the head and wings of a fierce dragon. A chimera's tail takes the form of a huge poisonous snake. These beasts have front feet resembling a dragon's claws and their hind feet are goatlike hooves.

Chimeras have several deadly natural weapons. The lion's head has strong jaws filled with sharp fangs and teeth. The goat's head has a pair of powerful horns. The snakelike tail ends with a snake's head that has a deadly, poisonous bite. Chimeras with dragon heads can also breathe fire or acid at their enemies.

Behavior: Most chimeras are dim-witted beasts. But those with dragon heads enjoy collecting treasure and sometimes attack nearby villages to steal gold. Chimeras normally live alone and spend much of their time hunting for food. These beasts are completely loyal to the wicked gods and wizards who made them. If a chimera's creator orders it to attack an enemy, it will do so without question.

Gorgons

Size:
5 to 5.5 feet
(1.5 to 1.7 m) tall

Habitat:
caves and old castles
near the sea

Diet:
mice, rats, rabbits,
frogs, fish, birds

Life Cycle: Gorgons are very rare. There have been very few reported sightings of them. However, this may be because few witnesses have survived encounters with them. It's thought that all gorgons are female. Some people believe they were once beautiful women cursed by the gods. Nobody knows if gorgons reproduce or how long they might live.

Physical Features: Gorgons often wear loose robes to cover their heads and hide their faces. But their true appearance can be seen up close. Gorgons have rough, scaly skin that is usually green or brown. They have jagged teeth, sharp fangs, and a forked tongue. Some gorgons have humanlike legs, but others have lower bodies resembling large snakes. A gorgon's most notable feature is the nest of writhing snakes on her head.

Behavior: Gorgons prefer living by themselves far from humans. They don't like intruders. Most gorgons are expert shots with bows. They usually first try to scare off intruders with a few well-placed arrow shots. Gorgons also have a powerful magical defense. One look from an angry gorgon's glowing red eyes will turn enemies to solid stone. Gorgons especially dislike warriors who invade their lairs to prove their courage. Unfortunately, some foolhardy young warriors don't realize the danger until it's too late. Gorgon lairs are often filled with stony statues of those who thought they could defeat these wicked creatures.

★ ★ ★
FANTASY ALL-STAR

Medusa is the most famous gorgon in history. According to ancient Greek myths, the hero Perseus killed Medusa. He avoided looking into her eyes by looking at her reflection in a golden shield. Perseus managed to cut off Medusa's snaky head and gave it to the gods as a gift.

Cerberus

Size:
6.5 to 7 feet
(2 to 2.1 m) tall

Habitat:
rocky plains and
lava fields

Diet:
none; Cerberus
does not eat

Life Cycle: Cerberus doesn't reproduce like most creatures. It isn't born and doesn't hatch from eggs. It is actually a cruel spirit that has taken physical form. Nobody is certain why or how it appears or how long it may haunt a location. It has rarely been seen by anyone who has lived to tell about it.

Physical Features: Cerberus appears as a huge, three-headed dog. Its muscular body is covered with short brown or black hair. Its feet are tipped with sharp 4-inch (10-centimeter) claws and each of the beast's three mouths is filled with wicked, gnashing teeth. It can also belch out large balls of fire to overwhelm its victims. The creature's piercing eyes also appear to glow with burning fire.

Behavior: Cerberus spends its time wandering rocky plains and lava fields near volcanoes. Nobody knows why it lurks in such locations. The beast may simply be looking for its next helpless victim. Cerberus may also be guarding secret entrances to its master's lair. It's possible that a wicked wizard raised Cerberus from the **Underworld** to be a personal guard dog.

★ ★ ★

FANTASY ALL-STAR

Fluffy is the name of a huge Cerberus-like dog from the popular book and film *Harry Potter and the Sorcerer's Stone*. Although Fluffy doesn't breathe fire, he fiercely guards the entrance to a secret room. However, Fluffy easily falls asleep whenever he hears music.

Underworld -- the place under the earth where ancient people believed spirits of the dead went

Sea Serpents

Size:
150 to 200 feet
(46 to 61 m) long

Habitat:
warm oceans

Diet:
fish, seals, squid,
sharks, whales,
human sailors

Life Cycle: Every 10 years female sea serpents lay up to 50 eggs in warm water near **tropical** islands. Serpent eggs are often discovered and eaten by other animals. For this reason, only a few eggs hatch successfully. Young sea serpents begin hunting for food and caring for themselves as soon as they hatch. Young serpents grow about 1 foot (0.3 m) per year. They don't reach adulthood until about age 150. It's thought that serpents can live up to 500 years.

Physical Features: Sea serpents have gigantic snakelike bodies. Their tough scaly skin is usually green or blue-green. Many sea serpents have dragonlike heads and mouths filled with deadly teeth. Some sea serpents may also have large fins that resemble a dragon's wings. Because of their dragonlike appearance, sea serpents are sometimes known as sea dragons.

Behavior: Sea serpents have huge appetites. They spend almost all of their time hunting for food. These creatures normally hunt large prey like whales or giant squid. A few people have reported seeing them hunt for seals near rocky coastlines. They occasionally attack human ships as well. They first coil their huge bodies around the ships and crush them. They then eat the sailors who jump into the water. Only a few sailors have been lucky enough to escape during a sea serpent attack.

tropical ⇢ having to do with hot
and wet areas near the equator

Kraken

Size:
more than 350 feet
(107 m) long

Habitat:
large caves on
the ocean floor

Diet:
fish, sharks, squid,
whales, human sailors

Life Cycle: Krakens are the rarest of all sea creatures. It's thought there are only one or two of these giant creatures in the world. Because they're so rare, nobody knows how they reproduce. It is also not known how long they can live. However, it's thought that these huge beasts grow very slowly and can live for hundreds of years.

Physical Features: Krakens resemble gigantic squids or octopuses. They are at least twice as big as most large merchant ships. Krakens have tough and rubbery skin. They also have incredible eyesight. Their huge 6-foot (1.8-m) eyes help them find prey in the darkest ocean waters. Krakens are best known for their 10 powerful **tentacles**. Krakens' gaping mouths are filled with dozens of huge, swordlike teeth that can kill prey in an instant.

Behavior: Krakens are among the largest and deadliest creatures in the world. Only a few people have ever seen one and lived to tell the tale. Krakens can sense when ships pass overhead. They like the challenge of fighting ships and enjoy the taste of human flesh. When a kraken attacks a ship, the beast wraps its huge tentacles around it. The kraken then quickly crushes the ship and pulls it under the ocean's surface. As it does this, the monster grabs doomed sailors and stuffs them into its gaping mouth.

FANTASY ALL-STAR

The gigantic kraken is a highlight of the hit 2006 film *Pirates of the Caribbean: Dead Man's Chest*. The film's villain, Davy Jones, sends the kraken after Captain Jack Sparrow because of an unpaid debt. The giant beast destroys several ships as it searches for Jack Sparrow.

tentacle ·-· a long, armlike body part some animals use to move, touch, or grab things

27

Legends Around the World

G Griffins

Griffins are commonly found in tales from Europe. "The Griffin" is one story in *Grimm's Fairy Tales* from Germany. The story tells of a young man who outwits a wise but deadly griffin. The story of "The Twelve-Headed Griffin" comes from Romania. It tells about a fight to the death between a young hero and a deadly griffin with twelve heads. Griffins also appear in stories from ancient Greek and Egyptian mythology.

K, S Krakens and Sea Serpents

Sailors have told frightening tales of huge sea monsters for thousands of years. Myths from ancient Greece and Scandinavia often describe deadly sea creatures that attack ships and sailors. In *The Natural History of Norway* the writer describes the kraken as a gigantic creature as big as an island. Another tale called "The Stronsay Beast" describes a huge sea serpent found on a rocky beach in Scotland.

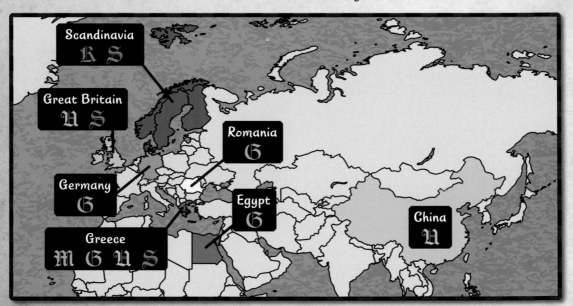

M Mythical Greek Monsters

The mythology of ancient Greece is filled with many fantastic creatures. Heroes in ancient Greek tales battled monsters such as harpies, gorgons, minotaurs, and the deadly, fire-breathing Chimera.

U Unicorns

Stories about unicorns come from several places around the world. Several ancient Greek myths feature unicorns. The tale of "The Hunter and the Unicorn" comes from China. And the story "The Fair Maid and the Snow-White Unicorn" comes from Scotland. Unicorns in these stories are often close friends and protectors of beautiful young women.

Test Your Knowledge

Do you know what to do if you encounter a harpy, unicorn, or gorgon? Do you feel ready to take on a minotaur or a deadly chimera? Test yourself with this short quiz to see if you're ready to become an expert on mythical beasts.

1 **To trap their prey, harpies will often:**

A. use magic to appear as beautiful women.

B. sing beautiful songs to cloud a person's mind.

C. set up a large table full of food.

2 **Wizards sometimes like to add phoenix _____ to their magic wands.**

A. ashes

B. tears

C. feathers

3 **You should never look into a gorgon's eyes because:**

A. it could turn you into solid stone.

B. you could lose your mind.

C. it's considered disrespectful.

4 **A chimera combines parts of which creatures?**

A. a horse, a lion, and an eagle

B. a lion, a goat, a dragon, and a serpent

C. a human, a vulture, and a bull

5 **A unicorn's horn can be used for making:**

A. strong healing potions.

B. powerful magic wands.

C. both A and B.

6 **Which group of creatures may be friendly toward people?**

A. Cerberus, chimeras, and krakens

B. griffins, pegasi, and unicorns

C. harpies, minotaurs, and gorgons

Glossary

foal (FOHL) ⇢ a young horse or horselike creature

ivory (EYE-vur-ee) ⇢ a hard, creamy-white material that makes up an animal's tusks or horns

lair (LAIR) ⇢ a place where a wild animal lives and sleeps

myth (MITH) ⇢ a story from ancient times

regenerate (ree-JEN-uh-rayt) ⇢ to make new

talon (TAL-uhn) ⇢ a long, sharp claw

tame (TAYM) ⇢ to train to live with and be useful to people

tentacle (TEN-tuh-kuhl) ⇢ a long, armlike body part some animals use to move, touch, or grab things

torso (TOR-soh) ⇢ the part of the body between the neck and waist, not including the arms

tropical (TRAH-pi-kuhl) ⇢ having to do with hot and wet areas near the equator

Underworld (UHN-dur-wurld) ⇢ the place under the earth where ancient people believed spirits of the dead went

Read More

DK Publishing. *Children's Book of Mythical Beasts and Magical Monsters.* New York: DK Pub., 2011.

Jeffrey, Gary. *Sea Monsters.* Graphic Mythical Creatures. New York: Gareth Stevens Pub., 2011.

Nardo, Don. *The Monsters and Creatures of Greek Mythology.* Ancient Greek Mythology. Mankato, Minn.: Compass Point Books, 2012.

Internet Sites

FactHound offers a safe, fun way to find Internet sites related to this book. All of the sites on FactHound have been researched by our staff.

Here's all you do:

Visit *www.facthound.com*

Type in this code: 9781491406908

 Check out projects, games and lots more at **www.capstonekids.com**

Index

Bellerophon, 13

Cerberus, 22–23, 29
    Fluffy, 23
chimeras, 5, 18, 29
    Chimera, 13, 28

gods, 18, 20, 21
    Zeus, 9, 13
gorgons, 20, 28, 29
    Medusa, 21
griffins, 5, 6, 28, 29

harpies, 5, 8, 9, 28, 29

krakens, 26, 28, 29

magic, 5, 8, 10, 15, 17, 20, 29
minotaurs, 5, 17, 28, 29

pegasi, 12, 29
    Pegasus, 13
Perseus, 21
phoenixes, 5, 10, 29

sea serpents, 5, 24, 28

stories and legends
    Harry Potter and the
        Sorcerer's Stone, 14, 23
    Egyptian myths, 28
    Greek myths, 9, 13, 21, 28
    Grimm's Fairy Tales, 28
    "King Phineas of Thrace," 9
    Pirates of the Caribbean:
        Dead Man's Chest, 26
    Scandinavian myths, 28
    "The Fair Maid and the
        Snow-White Unicorn," 28
    "The Griffin," 28
    "The Hunter and the Unicorn," 28
    The Natural History
        of Norway, 28
    "The Stronsay Beast," 28
    "The Twelve-Headed Griffin," 28

treasure, 18

unicorns, 5, 14, 15, 28, 29

weapons, 18, 20
wizards, 10, 15, 17, 18, 23, 29